All the World Loves a Puppet

JoAnne Alexander

Contents

Glove puppets	4
Marionettes	8
Shadow puppets	12
Water puppets	16
Bunraku puppets	20

People have been making puppets for thousands of years. Puppet shows are great fun, but they can also tell us a lot about a country's history and traditions.

Puppet shows are performed in theatres, behind screens, and on stage. People who perform with puppets are called puppeteers. They often require a lot of skill and training to operate the puppets.

This book will introduce you to some of the different kinds of puppets and puppeteers from around the world.

Glove puppets

Glove puppets fit over the hand of the puppeteer. The fingers of the puppeteer move the head and arms of the puppet. Glove puppets can be any kind of character, but probably the most famous are Punch and Judy, from England. These entertaining puppets are usually shown in a variety of comic situations. Their shows have been around for 300 years.

The puppeteer's fingers move the head and right hand.

The puppeteer's thumb moves the left hand.

This glove puppet is made of cloth and woollen thread.

5

Punch and Judy puppeteers are travelling street performers. People come to see Punch and Judy shows at parks, fairs and at the seaside. The puppet stage folds up and can be easily carried.

These children are enjoying a seaside Punch and Judy show.

The Punch and Judy puppeteer, called the professor, can put on a whole show alone. The professor moves two puppets at the same time, from underneath the stage.

Marionettes

Marionettes are puppets that hang from strings or wires above the stage. When the puppeteers pull the strings, different parts of the puppets move.

Marionette puppet shows are very popular in Italy, where they have been performed for over 500 years.

The strings are attached to cross bars.

This string moves the right hand.

This string moves the puppet's left leg.

The body of this marionette is made of wood.

Marionette plays often take place in theatres with lights and curtains. One play can have hundreds of characters. The puppets are dressed in decorative clothes.

The puppeteers stay hidden on walkways above the stage. Each puppeteer has to hold the cross bars of a marionette in one hand, whilst the other hand carefully pulls the strings that make the puppet move.

Shadow puppets

Shadow puppets are flat characters that have holes cut out to let light shine through. They are held on thin sticks or wires. Shadow puppets may look delicate, but they are made from stiff paper or leather and can last for hundreds of years.

Shadow puppet shows have been performed in India for more than 1,000 years.

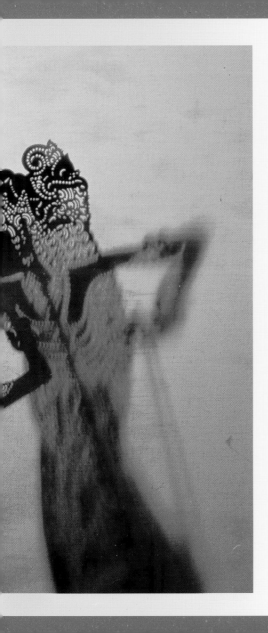

This shadow puppet is made of paper.

Holes in the puppet let the light shine through it.

This stick moves the arm.

This stick moves the body.

Some shadow puppet plays can last all night in the villages of India. Everyone knows the stories by heart. The puppets are introduced at the beginning of the show, but after that the audience only sees their shadows.

Lights from behind the puppets cast shadows onto the screen. The puppeteers are out of sight, behind the lights or below the screen. They dance, stamp their feet and jingle bells as they operate the puppets.

Water puppets

Water puppets stand on a platform that floats on water. The puppeteers gently move the puppets with strings and rods that are hidden underwater. The puppets glide gracefully and appear to dance on top of the water.

Water puppets have entertained villagers in Vietnam for more than 1,000 years. Long ago, farmers used their flooded rice fields as stages. The farmers got cold and wet as they put on the water puppet shows.

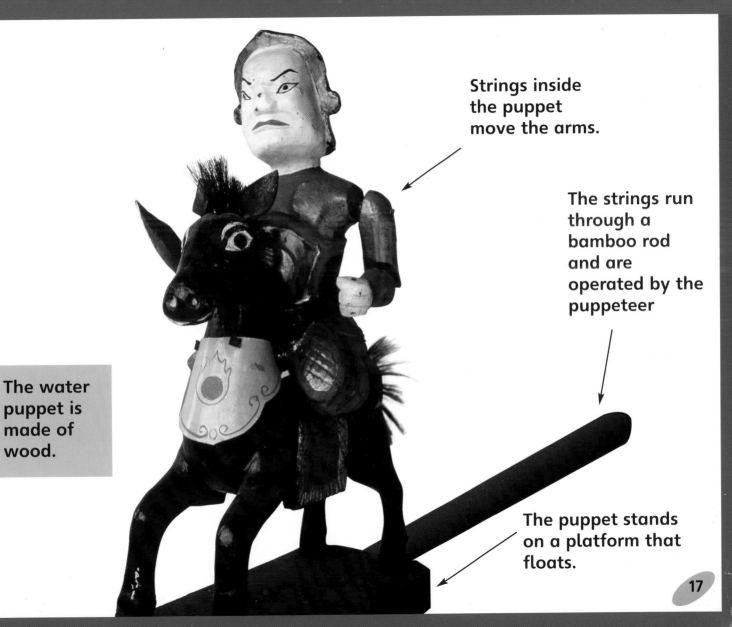

Strings inside the puppet move the arms.

The strings run through a bamboo rod and are operated by the puppeteer

The water puppet is made of wood.

The puppet stands on a platform that floats.

17

These days, water puppet shows are performed in shallow pools that can be set up anywhere. Dragon, frog and fish puppets often splash and squirt water at the audience.

Behind a screen, the puppeteers stand in the water. They wear wading boots to stay dry. A small band behind the pool plays music and sings the story.

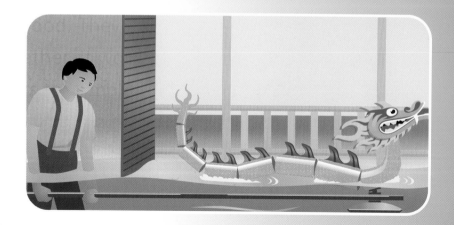

Bunraku puppets

Bunraku puppets have hidden rods and levers inside their baggy clothes. It takes three people to operate each bunraku puppet: a master puppeteer carefully moves the head, eyes, and right hand; one assistant moves the left hand, while another moves the legs.

This helper moves the puppet's legs.

The master puppeteer moves the head, eyes, and right hand.

This homemade bunraku puppet is made of cardboard.

This helper moves the left hand.

Bunraku plays began in Japan 300 years ago. Skilled woodcarvers and costume designers create the beautiful puppets. Puppeteers, storytellers and musicians study for many years before they can perform bunraku plays.

Bunraku puppeteers work on the stage with their puppets. The assistants are dressed in black, but the master puppeteer can be seen. The puppets never talk; instead, a narrator at the side of the stage tells the story.

Puppet shows – in their many forms – entertain people all over the world. For hundreds of years, puppeteers have spent many hours learning their craft so that the puppets they operate appear to come to life. This magical quality of puppets means that they are likely to be popular for many years to come.